DEDICATED TO

ALL LIGHT BEINGS
WORKING IN HUMBLE SERVICE
TO FURTHER MANKIND
IN ITS DEVELOPMENT
INTO FIFTH DIMENSION AND BEYOND

IN DEEPEST GRATITUDE
TO ALL MY FRIENDS
WHO KEPT ENCOURAGING ME
ON MY PATH

THANK YOU !

This page intentionally left blank

BE!

Texts for Transformation of the Self

channeled
by
Ruth Hildegard Henrich

First published by
Ruth Henrich Group
October 22, 2008

ISBN: 978-0-615-26077-8

Printed in the United States

1. Fiction 2. Inspiration 3. Psychology 4. Health & Science

ALSO BY RUTH HILDEGARD HENRICH

Into the Light – Prayers for transformation and meditation

What if…. – clarity for the doubtful

Healing Homes – living in healing spaces, creating sanctuaries

Art e ffects – transformational art

Fairy Gardens – creating paradises for fairies

IN LOVING MEMORY

OF

MARGARETHE GERTRUD BERG

This page intentionally left blank

FOREWORD

FALL 1999. I RECEIVED THE CALL. BE!
Not by phone - directly, in person by Uriel. I was
planting tulip bulbs in my garden in Sayn, Germany for
coming Spring. While envisioning the result, Springs'
fire-work of colors, a totally unexpected different
firework unfolded.

> BE! a clear loud voice.
> BE! a voice, right next to me.

I froze! Looking to my right, where the voice had
come from. There was no-one! Just clear air and a swift
breeze. No neighbours, nobody else around. I was
reassured alone. Shaking my head, ready for another
dig into the rich soil, which was waiting to embrace
another 5 tulip bulbs. There it was again!

BE! Loud and clear, even more firmly spoken
by a very pleasant deep voice. And in that very moment
I knew who spoke to me - it was Archangel Uriel,
awaking me to my true life's purpose.

MY HEART MADE A JUMP! With a big
plump I sat flat down. There amidst fresh dug earth,
spade still in hand, I was trying to understand and
comprehend what just had happened.

I sat there smiling, tears rolling down my face. I do not remember how long I sat like this. My heart was so light and I felt as if I was about to explode from joy. I felt Light shining from within.

BE! Literally knocked me off my feet. From one second to the next I was a different person. Or better said, I felt NEW.

What had happened? Why was I so very happy?

I FELT LIKE HAVING COME HOME after an enormously long time. Like ones true love returned after eons of absence. The same deep sense of warm embrace that touches each cell right down to the soul. My inside felt like after an unexpected wake up call, shaken to the core, leaving me unable to get back to the state I was in just a second ago.

I knew, from here a new life was starting. Nothing would ever be the same.

In the days and weeks following, answers to many spiritual questions came up. Having heard and read of such experiences by others, I consulted many books over the next years and talked to many people with somewhat similar experiences. Instead of finding my personal answer, every bit of information obtained, made my research more complex.

One beautiful gardening day in 2001 – two years and yards of books later - I realized that I needed to dedicate more time to my search for understanding. I had to find the answer in my deepest true Self.

No outside source could help. For one year I ended up spending 30-40 minutes every evening thinking and meditating in an empty church along the way home from work – pretending overtime worked. I literally scheduled my secret meditation time into every day. One month into this, I looked forward to each evening when I was lighting a candle, going into deepest meditation and asking my guides and higher self, Mother/Father God, universe PLEASE help me understand what is going on with me and where I am heading? And they answered and guided me!

MANY LIFE CHANGES RESULTED AS A CONSEQUENCE. All of them for the better, although some were hard and admittedly painful. It brought me to nearly exhausting my personal finances until I finally understood that I need to get all this information OUT, into the public, for everyone to read. The universe finally made me understand not to hold back all the information I was provided with. It was as if they said

WE HAVE NOT GIVEN THIS TO YOU TO KEEP IT TO YOURSELF, THIS WAS HANDED TO YOU TO SHARE WITH THE WORLD! DO IT! NOW!

I felt, like I was picking up my life where I had left it as a small child, decades ago. Slowly I started to slip back into my true Self. I wanted to make up for all the time missed.

IT WOULD TAKE UNTIL 2008, 9 years of dramatic life changes, parting from people which I had always considered having a true connection with. They simply rotated away and out of my life.

BE! thrown like a pebble into my calm lake of life, causing ripple effects of changes.
- had me part from a comfortable yet unexciting existence and made me go forward into Life.
- turned out to be a big cleansing on all levels of life.

BE! was the wake up call for my true lives' purpose.
- had me experience many adventures, countries and wonderful spiritual people.
- granted me the experience of my second crossing over in this life time, through an unexpected serious health issue.
- let me immigrate to Monterey Bay, California an area known to attract people on their path of transformation.

BE! had me make very pleasant, loving, exciting but also very strange and deeply disturbing even disrupting experiences. All to help me discover my true SELF, finding me MUCH stronger than I had ever imagined.

BE! a simple word changed my life, by making me follow my inner voice and truth, learning to trust my intuition.

I INVITE YOU TO LEARN from the coded teachings I have been given and instructed to pass on. Each one of you holds the key to their understanding.

THIS BOOK ASKS TO BE RE-READ many times over. Each time it will reveal new information. It feeds your hunger for knowledge and remembrance. It's teachings seed inventions that will further peoples. Your dormant creativity will be lit by sparks, blowing to you from another realm.

GET IGNITED.
LIGHT the world with YOUR true LIGHT.
Step out into the world and BE!

BE!

Lots of Light

Ruth Hildegard Henrich
Ambassador of Light

INTRODUCTION

Dearest beloved daughter we welcome you back to our midst. We have been longing to share relevant information with you, which we ask you to share with as many people as possible. Share the information we provide. In addition share the visions you were shown over the years. They are sent for the purpose of teaching *all*.

We demand you to write books on your visions and other information that we send through you. It is of utmost importance that people decode, what we have to say through your visions. You do not know who will hold these writings in their hands and discover greater wisdom buried inside them. The words we bring forth through you, hold keys that will unlock/awaken a multitude of energy beings presently incarnated on this planet. THEY NEED TO WAKE UP NOW !

Be assured that there will be many people in many countries embracing the information contained herein. It shall help them understand their own thoughts and dreams. It will further assist many people, reassuring them on their path.

It is not small, beloved daughter, what you are about to do. Do not think small of the wisdom, you shall share with the world.

Far too long your true identity and wisdom was hidden from the world. Stand up and be out there! Shine your Light for all other energies to see, so they can reach out to you. They have been waiting for you and your guidance. Be their Light in the stormy oceans of human life as it will soon be. Teach what we advise you to share.

Do not be afraid of what is heading your way. You are well prepared. Things that at first may seem strange, will make you remember past life experiences. You know perfectly what to do and how to react and act, when the time comes.

You have been well selected. Trust. All is in divine order. The timing is perfect. Let everything happen in its own time. We are with you. Be yourself – as fragile and sensitive as you are, as these senses will guide you on a safe way.

Remember yesterday morning, the huge foot formed by cumulus clouds! You will leave enormous footprints on this planet. You make and initiate changes for the better of this planet. This is your mission in this incarnation. You will spread true love all around, wherever you go. You have to meet with many important people to ignite the flame of true love for mankind and their spirituality. You shall set free many mentally imprisoned by blockage imposed on them by the churches and religions. It is to keep humanity from experiencing and knowing the truth, which lies within them. Your presence shall open their inward view and will make them realize their true reason for being here, on this planet, at this point in time.

After receiving this information I questioned the true nature of my purpose in this incarnation. I prayed and meditated for an answer "who am I?"

Following is the information received.

I AM

The answer was finally received December 2007 from my guides, totally unexpected while travelling. Here is what the ascended masters and angels say about their 'voice', whom they instructed to write the messages down:

> You are the one who comes
> With good news from afar,
> Across the water,
> With the strength to break up resistance.
>
> You are the one who lets
> mankind and physical world
> Arrive at their hidden truth
> And who makes them see through the
> illusions.
>
> You are the one who brings
> Advancement and happiness.
>
> You are the one who brings
> The necessity for transformation of the
> self.
>
> You are the one who brings information
> That will create great changes.
>
> You are the Ambassador of Light.

It took me months to be able to talk about this message.

It contains so much, which I needed to comprehend and digest myself first. Finally the puzzle pieces of my life come beautifully together.

Preceding above message were intensive prayers for being provided with further details and disclosure about my mission and purpose of this incarnation. As a result, I have compiled channeled prayers, provided by my angels and guides, with the instruction to share them.

These prayers have been published as

INTO THE LIGHT
Volume I
Prayers for transformation

May they help you as they have and are helping me.

Ruth Hildegard Henrich
Ambassador of Light

THIS PAGE INTENTIONALLY LEFT BLANK

THE ASHANTARA

Following is the channeled information received during the years 2003 through 2008, and written down as instructed for all ascending beings of Light. Please note that the following texts are channeled information. Since the source providing the information is different from subject to subject, the styles vary.

I have asked the energies/beings to reveal their names. They answered

> "We are many. We come forth as a group.
> You may call us **ASHANTARA**".

In the process of channeling the texts, the size of this group went from 33 to over 156 and it keeps growing as the subjects become more complex.
Some of the information had to be translated, as it was given in different languages (English, French, German, Latin, Sirian, Light Language and symbols unseen before).
How do I know the translations to be correct?
You are a light being yourself … you know the answer.

CHANNELING CHANGE

From the Lord God of my higher being I call forth now the presence and assistance of the Ascended Masters. Infuse me with the power, wisdom and love to communicate the words of change. I invoke the presence of the beings of the otherworld, underneath the Earth surface and the Ascended Masters and Angels above.

Following is their information to YOU

We are the ones to emphasize the change that needs to come about in this world.
We are many.
We are strong and powerful and have waited in humble service for the energies of mother Earth to raise, so our call can come through.

Since your childhood, Ambassador of Light, you were providing and feeding us information from your Third Dimensional world. In your sleep we called you back to report us the progress of this world. We have great news for you and all who read our words delivered through you. Be patient with yourself, as the words may not be understood at once. Much explanation will be needed. Gather in groups and re-read what we have delivered. Play with the information as it has layers of meanings, not just what is obvious to the eye.

Know that our words will create change within you. Feel into your heart.

If you feel you may not be ready at this time, put these words aside until you are. Our teachings will not be understood unless your heart is honest, pure and ready for them. To those who feel prepared to make the final step, we greet you courageous ones. Enjoy your journey and take notes of the changes happening.

CHANNELED INFORMATION

We are here together surrounding you to bring forth details which have not been revealed so far. It will be good to switch to handwriting as it will bring forth the energies better (it was all recorded in hand writing), besides your machines used to write down information may not be able to handle the energy with which we are coming in. We encourage you to also use the handwritten version for publication of this information *(a version in handwriting will be available).*

We understand that you are and will be feeling some sort of strain pain around your skull as we progress with the information. These are only the energies with which we come through. Your readers may experience similar symptoms. You shall be free of this pain as soon as our information flow stops coming through each time. Let us now begin with the details, which we ask you to share with the world.

Take a deep breath beloved daughter and rest.
Take another one.   And another.

Many people will be taught by you, Ambassador of Light, to guide others in the teachings. Many groups will form by your advice. They will carry the light forth around the globe.   This planet has been home to many entities of various energies. Some of them are visible to the human eye, others are only visible in the Fifth Dimension.

There are other dimensions beyond the Fifth Dimension which you can not comprehend at this time. Their energetic frequencies vibrate so high that human incarnation is not capable of receiving at this present time. But with your group ascensions forthcoming soon, you will see and understand what lays behind the veils and beyond the Fifth Dimension.

People of Earth rest your senses. There is much information coming forth that your senses, used to Third Dimensional processing, will not find rational explanations for. Your eyes will view images and movements that your mind has no references for. Your ears will hear sounds that your brain questions, but your soul will recognize.

Other senses like physical feeling through your skin will transform and no longer be as they are now. Touching will become an emotional sensation every time. Stay open for the new experiences, without questioning and analyzing them.

THE YOUNG ONES

Be in the moment and feel into every new experience. Play with them like children, new to the worlds ways, as that is what you are. You are the young ones in the Fifth Dimension. Stay open to all the new experiences and find pleasure in them. Playful you will learn fast to adjust and refine use of your new skills and abilities.

Before the shift there will be much confusion in the world. We ask you to be open to feel what is right and wrong information. Staying focused and centered through regular meditations is of great benefit. It helps you stay calm in the upcoming changes and chaos that will occur around you.

Soon your senses will receive information that your third dimension has no explanations for. Those around you, not ready for the shift, will be struggling, as nothing around them will make 'sense' anymore. Do not worry about them. It is their path they have chosen. They are not your responsibility. Only they can help themselves. You have done your share of bringing forward the message of Light.

Those who were able and ready to hear, have heard. Those who have not heard you, are of another frequency and have chosen a different path. They can no longer see or hear you. Include them in your prayers. Then let go. These beings are not your responsibility.

MINERAL KINGDOM

Dear reader of these words, open your higher chakras to receive this information passed on by our Ambassador of Light.

There underneath the surface, underneath the grass lies greatest treasure for human kind. The mineral kingdom is not what you so far have understood it to be. At one point in your past incarnations you were in the mineral and crystal kingdom yourself. You were there to experience the patience of being. You have experienced being in one location with highest presence of manifestation in crystal structure. Structures so complex that your scientists today still have not figured out the true making and meaning.

Minerals are like the machines you call computers in your third dimension. Only minerals are much more capable and versatile. They contain myriads of data and knowledge inside them. To tap into them, requires you to take your emotional shields down. Only the true hearted and pure can access and communicate with them.

There is everything you need for nourishment on all levels stored in the mineral kingdom. Power, wisdom and love beyond imagination.

The greatest truth about the mineral kingdom and its technological capabilities will be revealed once the Fifth Dimensional pyramids in Egypt/Giza will be visible to the world. Those of you who have the eye to see can see them located between and behind the three great pyramids from stone.

Another source provided further details on crystals in another chapter

HIEROGLYPHS I

The hieroglyph symbols left by the Ancients contain the keys for using this technology stored within the Fifth Dimensional pyramids. Refined frequencies such as sound, thought and emotions are the keys to this great wisdom. Only the ones pure at heart will be able to tap into the knowledge of the Ancients.

Know that YOU are the ones who buried this wisdom. WE CALL TO WAKE YOU! Wake to retrieve the knowledge and tools you have hidden for yourselves. That is the reason why the symbols and structures have always been fascinating to human kind. You have hidden the keys from yourself, not only in this evolutionary state but many times before.

The symbols resemble frequencies which trigger inside you remembrance of deepest ancient knowledge. Deep down inside of your being you remember your connection with them and their true meaning.

We see you in great joy and happiness once you start to remember. The truth is hidden in the open view. It only takes the pure hearted eye and mind to understand and comprehend the beauty of its multi layered meaning.

More details were provided on this subject in a later session

BODIES

The density of the planet Earth at present creates major dis-functions in your cell memory. As a consequence most part of your DNA and brain cells are unable to be used in Third Dimension. The cells your scientists have labeled 'dormant' will be fully functional in the Fifth Dimension. Your capabilities are about to perform a major leap together with your senses.

All your living body cells are part of your brain. Your brain is not limited to the skull area. Finally after decades of research your scientists discovered that when you feel pain in your toe (furthest distance from your brain) your brain cells signal back to your foot to move away from the pain creating situation. Your scientists concluded quantum science as explanation. The foot sensation is moved back in time BEFORE the brain in fact sends the impulse.

Let us tell you, that your scientists were wrong. They made a wrong assumption - human brain is not solely confined to the skull. To fully comprehend true connections inside the human cell nucleus, it will take the shift into Fifth Dimension. It takes a much higher calibration of your fine tuned systems on an electron level. The connections will run at such high speed inside your brain cells (all over your system) and body systems. Such would have destroyed your bodies in the Third Dimensional density.

It takes your ascension into Fifth Dimension to understand what you are truly capable of.

Beings of the Light you are so much more than what you presently can imagine. You are almighty creators. You are pure thought. Your thoughts create your 'realities'. You have been living on a 'holographic deck' and are standing at the brink of realization.

Many of you have already experienced that their body and skin feel less dense. Some even see or feel themselves turning partly translucent. This is the beginning of the shift into Fifth Dimension. In connection with this experience several of you feel the sensation of growing to 8 or 10 feet height during their meditations.

Let us tell you that You are feeling your Fifth Dimensional body. Embrace your new you. It will be vibrant and rejuvenated. You, the Young Ones shall be youthing.

We understand this is hard to comprehend at this point in time. We encourage each and everyone of the energies and beings reading this material, brought forth by our Ambassador of Light, to start singing or thinking sound. Get used to singing tunes of harmony. Listen to the birds. They are messengers between the worlds. This is why the ancients made the connection of winged messengers, angels.

Angel 'wings' are forms of high calibrating energies swirling around them, similar in appearance to the infinity symbol. The easiest to describe and picture such energy was through feathers much like bird wings.

The ancient ANCH symbol has more dimensions than usually depicted in your limited Third Dimension. In all its dimensions the Anch consists of two energies flowing in elliptical infinity swirls interwoven and connected in the heart chakra. If you wish, you can see the human body as materialized by thought within these two interwoven energies. The beauty is that the link is able to shift between all chakras, such creating a grand kaleidoscope of experiences on the energetic level.

Now you understand why energy never can get lost. It merely shifts into another frequency. At free will you can lower the frequency and thus exist in a dimension of your choice. It also allows space travel.

How limiting is the use of words in your present dimension. It is so inadequate to express the full range of experiences and thoughts but especially emotions. You will find great pleasure in the use of transcendental information flow. It is faster and much more efficient than any of the tools humans have created to mimic this feature they carry inside them…just like all your technical tools are copies of your senses and capabilities. You copied your eyes by means of cameras and TVs.

You copied your ears through radios and telephones. Once in the Fifth Dimension you will not need any of those crutches any longer. Talking will become very silent, yet very informative as all information (word, thought and imagery) can be send regardless of distance to any recipient.

Understand that the hieroglyphs have a different meaning than what you invented them to mean. They are no words. They are sound and complex imagery combinations with a multitude of layers in meaning. Additionally you assume you know where to start "reading" them. Let us tell you that the information is multi layered and is to be understood from all angels of the dimensions. Similar to human's old ways of recording music in carved lines on black disks. Without the proper mechanics / machine it remains a black disk with carved lines not revealing what it contains.

Hieroglyphs' are meant to be scanned with your chakra frequencies to reveal their meanings. They will sing and swirl in the sky once seen with the right "device" and "key". Your third eye will see and your heart feel and so resonate their meaning. Once you absorb and comprehend their meaning with your finer Fifth Dimensional senses you will remember. The simplicity and beauty will make you weep of joy. Together they are grand harmonious accords that will trigger your memories. We wonder why no one ever thought of them as frequencies of music and imagery. Your third dimension is so limiting.

Looking at single musical notes does not reveal the beauty of a symphony, nor touch your soul like the symphony does – understand that your present understanding of the ancient hieroglyphs is like looking at single music notes and trying to grasp the full range of a symphony on all levels (hearing, feeling and emotion).

People of Earth we want you to unlimit yourself. We are here to awake you and to break you free from your chains.

Sing to the Sphinx! Is our message to our Ambassador of Light. She (sphinx) is the picture in its original structure of a whole being. It is man, it is female and creature too. All its senses are sharpened and hightened. All is in perfect harmony, open to receive. Yet it is located in one firm spot, just like a mineral inside the Earth. And YES you may have guessed already, there are major crystals underneath the sphinx. Digging in the sand will not reveal them, as they calibrate so high that they can only be seen by Fifth Dimensional beings.

We have shown you the capstone in its present location. You hold the key to move it, together with three other beings. When the time has come you shall gather in the location and initiate the relocation.

The location of ancient Egypt's structures changed after eons of planetary movements. But mother Earth will know to stretch herself and balance the energy fields right.

Many energy workers are presently working on realigning Mother Earths chakras and reopening Vortexes. They travel great distances in frequent intervals to accomplish this mission. Many have left their families and homes in order to assist in this task.

The water is out of balance and causes great turbulence on mother Earths inner being. The waters need to be rebalanced. It takes a lot of magnetic force fields to create stability with this unbalanced water, which is nothing but the mechanisms of mother Earths electro magnetic information transport.

The major portals all over the planet are the openings into which highly evolved beings tap in and can enter, to exchange information, cause and start changes on the planet. Workers deep down inside the Earth are creating balance after balance. Now is the time that great final changes are needed in order to heal and cleanse Mother Earth. It will be a great shaking for those who will not calibrate at higher speed of Fifth Dimension.

Mother Earth is getting lighter in weight as she is getting hotter, speeding up in her vibrations. The ocean waves, her breath, will get rough and high as she is birthing her new self. Huge tidal waves and rains will cleanse the surface, just as it has happened several times before.

A crystal shield in the outer atmosphere, has nearly been completed. Some of you with higher vibrations are able to see the rainbow of colors in the sky. This crystal shield is part of the crystals that have surfaced in the last years. This protection shield will assist Mother Earth's shift. Know the crystals are protecting you. Higher thought forms and energetic beings are protecting you.

The moon is showing something like an atmosphere since some time, which has build up in the last years. It is not an atmosphere but also a crystal shield. The moon itself is helping balance Earth magnetism. Just like Sirius has it's counter balancing small planet, Earth has it's Moon.

Many of you have wondered about the travel to moon by your people. The images shown to you, many immediately sensed as 'unreal', untrue. Know that they were! The findings on the planet were so un-explainable, that in order to avoid mass panic on Earth, the images were manipulated down to what human mind could handle at the time. Interestingly enough former scientists on the project, now start to write about the real findings of this mission. (for more insight we refer you to: NASA the truth about the mission to the moon)

WAKE UP CALL

Wake up people of Earth! Trust your intuition and feelings. Do not take imagery provided to you for what your scientists explain to you. Many letters after a name does not guarantee the truth.

Go inside yourself and FEEL what is shown to you. You KNOW what is true. Do no longer be afraid to openly talk about what it is you are sensing. You will be surprised how many others feel the same. Do no longer deprive yourself from confirmation ! Confirmation of your true identities and knowledge.

THE GOLDEN LIGHT

We have come together today to teach and instruct about the Golden Light. Not many do understand that there is Golden Light coming through to the ones which have chosen to incarnate at this time as the leaders and teachers of the new world.

They shall teach the light beings following prayer:

> In the name of the mighty
> victorious presence of God,
> I AM in me and my Holy Devine Self.
> I call to the Ascended Masters, Angels
> and the Golden Ray of Resurrection.
> *(visualize bathing in the Ray. Fill your auric body with its light and every cell of your physical, mental and emotional body.)*
> I ask you to _____.
> Please let my call be multiplied
> for all who are in need.
> I accept it done, this hour in full power,
> according to the will of God.

Note:
under the title "Into the Light" channeled prayers have been published.

Many of you awakening will begin to see Golden Light beings. They can show themselves and appear in various means in your life. They shall be visible to the Eye.

I asked for clarification of the term eye, since they capitalized it, but the Ashantara would not disclose if they mean human eye, third eye or camera lenses. So I interpret that you, dear reader, will know how this relates to you .

They present themselves obvious through your senses in the present moment. Those who let their Lemurian senses guide them, shall feel their presence. You will *know* their presence.
You will *know* when they are under your feet - inside the earth, in the air in front of you... you can feel their energy pulse.

The Golden Light Beings are pure loving thought energy, pulsing into your life as you keep your channels open and evolve in frequency. We ask those who hold proof to come forth and show the world what they were gifted with.

Know that the energies shown are not the actual Golden Light Beings themselves. The energies your Eye sees are loving thoughts send to you, to confirm your path.

The golden Light Beings are so high in frequency and light that your present human dense form is unable to handle the light and energy they emit. Not to damage you prematurely, these Beings are sending you their loving thought forms to assure you of their existence and presence.

It is one of the laws of frequency that the higher realms can see into your reality but you can not see into theirs.

All your dense bodies can handle at this time are small glimpses into mirrors of the true existence of the Golden Light.

There will be those of you who want to force progress. Be warned, it shall harm you to proceed prematurely. Know that there will be many of you, not able to handle what shall reveal itself. Their human minds will not be able to process the information, unless they decide at free will which path to follow. Do not interfere. Allow.

The Ascended Beings, walking among you in your density, have chosen to take your hands, to guide you through the turbulences that frequency shifts bring. Take their hands and hold on. Trust them. They know their way and have a stable connection with source and their home planets through strong and stable energy beams.

These Beings hold the codings that will open the gates. The contracts for unfolding the sequence of occurrences was made long ago. The codes will become known to them shortly before needed. It is in great beauty how everything will unfold.

LAUGH PEOPLE OF EARTH !
YOU HAVE COME A LONG WAY
AND THE LIGHT WILL SUCCEED !
KNOW THAT YOU KNOW !
YOU FEEL IT.
TRUST WHAT YOU FEEL.

AWAKENING I.

Mother Earths changes are passing through - what you call *time* - faster and faster. It is happening at greater speed – you consider it such and by this expression - as that is, how you feel it happening.

Changes are coming forth faster, as more and more energy Light Beings awaken on this planet.

Thought, light and sound are the triggers for the awakening. It is the big awakening of many people. Even those who yesterday considered many of our energies simply as hocus-pocus, suddenly see, feel and understand. It will come as a shock to these people, as suddenly right is wronged and vice versa. It literally will turn their understanding of the world upside down.

It will become more and more a desire, a yearning and need, for many of you Light Beings to live secluded, like hermits, for long periods of time. You need to retreat, regroup all your energies. You love to be out and teach, but you also need time alone.

Adjusting to the new frequencies will force many to rest for longer periods of time. Strict adherence to frequent meditations and prayers will be greatly beneficial in the adjustment to the new frequencies. This will assist you in staying balanced in your emotions.

Then there will be periods of time in which you will enjoy being around like minded energies. You will teach many Light Beings – but also need to listen to us, calling you back into contemplation and rest.

Additionally such times will find you in an almost state of sleep, without hunger.

FIND AND CONFIRM YOURSELF

Beloved you have come into this incarnation at your own request. You passed through many new experiences as a small child, while getting used to the Third Dimensional density of this planet. You learned how things are viewed, how they are named, you learned to experience emotions, operate and work with your human senses....

When you incarnated you forgot what you knew, except for the essence of your mission. It is part of incarnating on planet Earth, that you forget due to its density most of your wisdom and knowledge.
The wisdom and knowledge is not lost, you just can not access it. Your knowledge and wisdom of how powerful you truly are, would create major disruption. You simply can not go to planet Earth with all your wisdom. It would hinder you in experiencing and learning what you have come here to learn and experience.

You never loose connection with source and so, once you are ready in your development and stage of incarnation, you can ask source to grant remembrance. Ask for it, in your prayers and meditation.

Dear Light Being, we warn the light-hearted ones. Be careful and fully aware of what you ask for. Do not ask for full remembrance on all levels at once. Take your time to re-discover what you have known before, as it can create fear.

As soon as you get into fear or sense you are heading there, call upon Archangel Michael for protection, to surround you in white light.

Avoid fear, as it feeds the dark. Do not become easy game for them. Stay in the Light. There are many healers on the planet at this time to assist you, should you go too fast. Be careful and patient dearest, everything is happening for you in perfect timing.

You and your guides and angels designed a detailed plan for your incarnation before you came here. Many of you get impatient. You have seen a glimpse of what being enlightened means. You seek for reinforcement, for miracles and wonders to confirm what you sense, feel and sub-consciously know. You ask if what you sense really exists. You are asking from a place of doubt. You ask, is this really real?

It may come as a shock to the others when you tell them that all they know as Third Dimensional 'reality' is in fact not real. This so called 'reality' does not exist. It is a dream. It is thought. Your experience of 'reality' is a manifestation of thought, to allow You the experience(s) you can only make here (such as time and space).

There are many of you incarnated at present who can see through the illusions. These Beings faced major problems when coming in as a child. They are the higher Beings of Light, that have important missions to fulfill. They remember and hold the codes, the final keys.

When they came into their incarnation, they had to learn to understand the common terms, as they would 'see' everything as what it truly is – pure energy.

Their eyesight is very different. They have the capability to see through all matter 'reality' and know it is an illusion. In addition they can create and manifest thought into matter by seeing inwardly. They see more colors than others. See auras, Devas, grid lines and Earth energies. They have extremely powerful healing energies and can reanimate Beings. Many of them have plenty of experiences in reanimating other energies.

Among other unusual non-human things they can walk through "matter", like walls and closed doors, but had to learn not to do it. They blocked their knowledge how to do it. Their mind works by manifesting thoughts, which they learned to block. Many think they lost the knowledge, but it only is non-accessible in the Third dimensional density. Once these Beings were comfortable in their incarnated body they operated as expected by their respective surroundings (family, society). Until they reach the point of their incarnation where their codings are set to re-open. Then their memory will return: who they truly are, their mission and their powers.

Many of them have spent much time re-discovering their wisdom and gifts. How to apply and use them in Third Dimension, step by step, very gently.

Even more time was invested to identify how they can use these gifts in meaningful ways without disruption of other life's, yet accomplish their mission of this incarnation. The time has come for these beings to step up and BE! Know and be, who they truly are.

Before they came in, most of these special Light Beings have asked for serious health issues or abuse at very young age, to give them the freedom to be in themselves and secluded. These events (health issues) at the start of their incarnation allowed them to focus on their mission from the beginning. It took them out of the 'normal' human routines and processes, allowing them to spend time in seclusion.

During that time they focused on developing certain talents, meditation, prayer and staying centered – all of which will needed for their important tasks once the frequency shift starts.

These Beings are the strong centered leaders that have overcome bodily experience for strengthening intend, mind and soul.

To give the human mind something it can relate to: Julius Caesar, suffering epilepsy, was said to have been chosen by the heavens – it is such health issues we talk about.

NOURISHMENT

WATER

You need to take care of having good pure drinking water. Drink frequently as our energies can only download easily when your human body is in an as close to perfect condition/state as possible. It is much easier to download the electrically charged energies into a healthy body with plenty of receptives in liquid form. The information flow is easier.

This is the first very important task of all Light Beings. Ensure you drink enough pure water. Mother Earth and the Crystal kingdom shall supply you with purest water. It is your duty to check the ways your drinking water is treated and stored. Water is the most precious source of nourishment for your present bodies. It shall further be of great importance in other means as you shall find out.

This planet is the only one with immense masses of water – in liquid, gas and solid form. There are many solid varieties of water, human kind has not even discovered yet due to the density on Mother Earth. What you consciously are aware of at this time are rain, streams, rivers, lakes and the oceans as liquid form. As gas form you know clouds and fog. As solid you know ice (glaciers, the poles, hale).

Also crystals contain water that replenishes itself. Crystals can store so much more than you know.

Water is a conductor. It lets electrical energy pass with great ease and picks up thought patterns. Once your Light Being scientists have found the way to pulse the electric energies of thought through water in a way unharmful to other beings – not intended as recipient – you will discover how easy energy and information can be transported and send over great distances.

Proper storage of water is very important. Water picks up surrounding energies, good and bad. Make sure to purify your water before drinking it. Change the energies to positive before allowing them to enter your human system.

Use following numerology for this:

With your right hand circle clockwise
three times over the water (food)
For each circle you make, say: **9 9 5**

This changes the energies and takes out any negativity. Sending your source of water loving thoughts will accomplish the same.

FOOD

Dear Light Beings. Know that your human body picks up frequency and energy through food. All positive frequencies to resonate with your higher systems are contained in food, mainly water, crystals from the mineral kingdom and further qualities in a variety of ways. Therefore pay closest attention to taking in well grown nature sources. Your body was not meant to take in animal source other than for dedicated soul experience. The ancient knew of this wisdom and held sacred rituals.

Why have you forgotten of these rituals? You were to absorb your animal brothers frequencies only for gaining their strength for one experience. You have turned this into a daily intake of unclean slaughtered animal brothers without going through ritual and giving thanks to their spirit.... Therefore the absorbing of your brothers, the animals has become unclean for you. Don't you know that you pick up the negative frequencies each time? People of Earth you have bought into darkness' false stories.

There are the others of you which eat only fruit and vegetables, but fail to balance it well. Don't you know that you need to balance the type and area of growth of fruit and vegetables? Do not eat too much of those growing in the air ... if you eat these, balance them with vegetables and fruits growing inside the Earth (soil). It shall ground you again.

Grounding will become more and more important in the upcoming times of change. To stay grounded you shall eat fruit that grows inside of Mother Earth, so you stay linked to her. Other fruit makes you beings too airy.

If you seek spiritual connection, go on a diet that contains much air growing fruit and vegetables. This will help you get connected. Make sure to ground yourself afterwards with Earth fruit and vegetables.

If you seek to increase your energy for tasks that require a lot of strength, do not eat at all for a time. Thus your body is free to use all energy for the purpose. Such purpose can be healing or muscle use. Some of you understand the value where it provides for further detailing of energy frequencies.

We are not saying to stop taking in food. Do not hesitate to eat whenever you feel weak. Only the strong can refrain from food intake. Although some of you would greatly benefit in healing through absence of food. Liquid balance is important to ensure proper information flow within your system and with source.

Dear Light Beings, be aware of your own healing powers. Listen to your human bodies and bring them back into balance.

You have accepted a state of imbalance as your balance. Wake up to the awareness. Let your divine essence guide you to re-balance your inner systems. Feel into your body when taking in food. Feel what is right. Watch your bodily reactions. Your human body communicates beautifully with you, you just have to listen.

Listen to its guidance and you can not go wrong.

CRYSTALS

You will further discover that **crystals** are the perfect storage form for water- and any other liquid resources. However, before you will be able to do this, there will be major research and new technologies brought forward by our crystal beings.

It is wise to invest in crystals. They will be highly sought after in the future. Crystals will be involved in means of communication – similar as you use them already today in your computers, TV monitors, flat screens, cars, aircrafts and all sorts of electronic devices.

Not many know that crystals can change their appearance and properties. They can change by intent – thought. Crystals can be liquid (like in your screens – touch your computer screen and see the 'water'rippels), appearing solid or as a gas.

The crystal kingdom is much more versatile than presently understood. The properties of the various crystaline structures combined with the properties of light, color, density and temperature, result in a yet undiscovered magnitude of possible beneficial uses. Your future transportation will be through crystals, light and intend.

We have started to lecture on the field of the multitude of crystal energy use. The crystal kingdom will be the future source for your entire transportation needs. The crystals themselves will teach you how to use them best for what purpose. Until then we shall only reveal so much: crystals are your future solution for most energy problems.

Men will learn how to grow crystals with specific properties. Once the means of this technology and purpose programming within the crystal structures are known and understood, a multitude of new tools and technology, unthinkable before will be 'invented'. Actually they will be very similar to our present tools in the Fifth Dimension and are used by ET, only simpler. Also know that it necessitates a certain mindset and purity of thought to program and use these tools, as your minds will be their steering / power source. This may sound unthinkable today, but in time you start using them with ease. You will wonder why you never thought of it before and will consider all previous methods 'stone-age' technology.

Know that the crystal kingdom is the one protecting planet Earth during its big shifts coming up in the next years. You will suddenly understand the total beauty of the protective sources the crystal kingdom has been and will be providing for you. You will as human kind be eternally thankful to those Beings and energies presently incarnating in the crystal form. Being of their mind, as all of you have had an incarnation in the crystal form as well, you will understand the great beauty of it all.

The crystal Beings are very powerful in exchanging and utilizing thought form and information. They all are interconnected on a higher plain thus being able to draw resources from every and all other crystal beings. Their interconnectedness on this higher level of existence allows materialization through thought form in one of the most efficient manners.

Crystals are the only true form for storing information secure and unmodified over very long periods of time. Highly evolved beings can store information through intend of thought into crystal beings, who will hold it for them until another energy source like the original programming source unlocks the information by codes. No other being is granted access into the stored information.

The crystal skulls hold a message from all crystal and other Beings to the Light Beings in the world. Only those Beings who hold the codes, understanding and knowledge can tap safely into the securely stored information contained inside the crystal skulls. Only those with the proper codes are invited into the crystal kingdom wisdom and "technology".

The means of HOW to get into the stored information inside the crystal skulls requires codings stored inside the Light Being of pure heart and mind. The security measures built into these *libraries of the light*, are phenomenal once understood.

Know that everything is safe, as Beings with any less intention than totally pure, can not, we repeat this, CAN NOT enter the crystal kingdom knowledge. Whoever attempts to get into close proximity on an energy level, will either have to transform deep down in it's atoms of being, and thus transform into pure love or they shall stay outside forever... gazing at crystals as something simply material.

The lines of energetic mind crossings are very fine and VERY sharp.
Beings not holding the required codes on a sub-atomic level within them, will not unharmed cross the line into the knowledge of the mineral kingdom.

So much for now from the crystal kingdom.

Talk about cutting edge technology!

BEING AND BEINGS

What do we need to know about foreign species visiting our planet?
The ugly ghostly aliens your science fiction authors dream of, may exist somewhere in the universe - maybe in another reality or time line. Understand that everything thinkable by spirit comes into existence - yes everything. So be mindful of your thoughts. Every thought you have, creates a reality, including the creation by thought of beings and energies into existence – of whatever properties they may be.

Most humans fail to understand their own thought patterns. Every thought you have, has been in existence on another plain already, as that is from where it is coming/drawn to you. It is your free will on this planet that allows them in or leaves them out.

No highly advanced intelligent 'alien' species interested in experiencing your human life form would come here in an ugly appearance hindering their research. Never forget that you – you the human Being – are spirit incarnated for the experience of bodily feelings and emotions. The aliens you search for are already among you. You are the ones you are looking for. You have either incarnated into this life form and experienced growing from a small into an adult human being, or you have walked into an existing life form.

Nothing happens by chance. All is based on wise plans by your energetic highest self and all its facets and partner parts. Thought form on the other plain is not done by only one being. BEING as matter of fact has an entirely different meaning in this realm. BEING there is understood as ONENESS. Your higher energetic self is interconnected with ALL the other energies, of all the experiences ever in all incarnations ever. So you do not differentiate between certain parts of your higher self.

There is no certain area for the heart or the brain. Your higher self is all one with everything and all energies of pure light and love. So when your higher self uses let's say it's *brain,* all beings, fauna and flora included, is what your thought draws from. But this isn't all… the heart with all its emotional remembrance is linked, as everything is linked in this realm.

On the highest light energy levels of being you feel, sense, see, hear, taste, from all energetic memory and present experiences (by all beings incarnated) …And you feel, see and sense it all at once.

Your being in this plain is like the air, charged to the maximum with Light energy and love. Understand that you can be breathed into another Being, but you are not only the air this Being breathes in, you are also the Being itself. You become part of it and share all its experiences, feelings and emotions. You are everywhere at once, inside and outside, above and below.

You hover, stand, sit, live deep inside the Earth, fly, shoot through the sky like a shooting star…. AND you are FULLY aware of all these experiences, feelings and emotions. You truly ARE in the NOW. You PULSE with the universe… as you are ONE with the universe.

We understand that this may be hard for you to comprehend. But once you get to the feeling point of this experience, as a memory in your deepest mind, you will KNOW and you will REMEMBER. You will remember who you truly are, where you have been, where you come from now and where you are heading.

This energetic BEING of ONE, which you are part of, always searches for more knowledge. It does not rest. Never. It always longs for finding new experiences and more wisdom. Thus the goal you attempt to reach, in fact gets further out of reach every time you learn and experience something new. The more you add to your wisdom the further away moves your goal of completion.

Imagine two hills and the valley in between. Your goal is to reach the other hill, the one you see. But as soon as you get there you see another hill and want to go there, not remembering that it was the place where you initially started. On an energetic level it means you are attempting to reach the other end of a RING. By going further and further your initial perspective changes and your goal to reach a certain spot on the ring changes.

Your goal no longer is to get to the other spot. Your goal becomes the way of doing so. Energetically the picture for this is, you are in one spot on a RING energy and want to reach another spot on this RING energy. But in attempting to go there your energy tips over in adding experiences, thus leaving the RING energy, tipping over backwards and coming around in an ∞ …

So here is your explanation for the symbol of eternity, the horizontal EIGHT… which actually is more a movement of energies than a static symbol. Understand the infinity, horizontal EIGHT, as Light energy moving at high speed and picking up more speed each time it reaches the outer end of each RING.

Understand that pure energy can only increase, become more. It does not die or get lost.

The higher the energy 'speed' increases the less dense the form will become. This is contradicting your present understanding of physics, which expects a compressing state. Truth is that the energy with increasing speed, becomes less and less dense until it becomes invisible ONENESS with everything.

You now understand better that being incarnated in your present energy form, requires a lot of control on your side, as you are constantly lowering your energy frequency to a much lower state.

It is that which guarantees you being visible in this realm and density. But know that in truth you are both, visible and invisible. It is your free will alone that can manifest your state of being at any given time.

Understand that you are not this body that carries around your mind on this planet. You are so much more. The use of your brain resembles a perfect example. 90% are unused while on this planet in Third Dimensional Density – those 90% you are using outside of this realm. You are so much more than you presently can comprehend.

BALANCING MOTHER EARTH

Most of you are here at this time to assist Mother Earth in the shift and to help her balance her energy vortexes. Many of you Light Beings who incarnated at the present time on this planet are here for balancing of Light energy.

Mother Earth has various huge energy vortexes through which energies (like you), information and beings can enter into this density. With all the big shifts going on, on this planet, the gravitational speed and magnetic pole shift, a regular circular spin would be impossible. With all the dark forces fighting against their extinction in the Middle East vortex, a need for a balance on the opposite side of the planet was essential.

Do you, Llight Being, reading these words, still wonder why you are WHERE you are? Many of you 'balancers' have been called to move to California. You have moved here from far away countries. If you did not follow your inner voice, demanding you to come here, then the universe created another life scenario that forced you to come here. You have been called to this place to balance the energies working in the Middle East.

It is you, who will be travelling around this planet many times over – we will make you go wherever your balancing energy is needed.

Many of you feel different in their old areas, where they used to live. The air and energies there feel stuffy or used up. You are not able to spend much time in these areas anymore without becoming very uncomfortable. This is caused by your raised energies/frequencies which no longer are supported in these areas.

Feel where you truly feel good and listen to your body symptoms. This is the beauty of your human body. Many of your organs have many more functions than is obvious and known. Listen to your bodily symptoms when travelling and moving about the planet. You may cross energy lines and magnetic fields that energize you. There are certain spots or areas that make you feel drained. Simply follow your body signals and prefer the spaces/areas that make you feel good and let you vibrate in your own higher frequency. (We ancient Egyptians and other cultures left planet into such higher realm where we feel better and are safe)

When you drive around – feel into the areas you come through. Are there lines of energy that create goose bumps, shivers or cause your hair to stand up? Do your chakras start to spin faster (a feeling of shaking like during an earthquake)? When walking, do your foot chakras start to tingle?
Keep training your awareness for your bodily feelings.

Most important go out into nature and feel how it makes you feel. Feel the air, the wind, and the sounds. This of course implies that you do go out into nature. It is enough to walk in a small park.

Make your feet touch the ground – don't always drive around. Walk. Breath in fresh air, not always filtered, air-conditioned air. Fill your lungs with fresh air.

When you live in a big city we highly recommend to spend days in the country side each month. When you meditate, call in the feeling of filling your lungs with fresh air, as experienced during your outside stays.

As mentioned earlier, the Light energies among you will find a greater need in the future to live in the country, closer to nature. Also earlier we mentioned that you may experience a feeling of being drained. This does not contradict what we have said before. It only proofs that your energy is so high, that certain areas don't allow you being your full energetic you. That is what provides the experience of feeling drained. Your energetic body can not spin at it's rate, to hold your visible manifestation of your bodily incarnation. If you stay in such areas, your visible manifestation deteriorates (becomes sick) to a point where it exits the body (dies). This may take what you presently sense and comprehend as TIME.

From our perspective this only feels this way, as it includes such a huge magnitude of energy frequency changes on the smallest level of atoms and nucleus inside your manifested bodily incarnation. Since you control each and every nucleus' change, that is what makes you experience a sense of time.

There is a lot of highest wisdom involved going through the transformation from the bodily manifestation into the unbodily energetic being of oneness. Of course one may ask why don't we just switch from one state into another. Please understand that the difference in frequency is tremendously large. There may be a time where you simple dematerialize and rematerialize in a different form of experience willingly at ease. But before such can be reached, there are many emotions to be felt and many other experiences added.

Know that nothing is ever lost. All experiences made are stored and add to the foundation of your wisdom. Nothing gets ever lost. As this foundation becomes stronger and stronger your goal of reaching a final completed state moves farther and farther away from you.

Fully understanding what we just said means, you love being in the NOW rather than getting somewhere or to finish something.

You enjoy BEING.

BE!

MIND MANIPULATION

They will feel a great need to eliminate electronic devices such as phones, radios, TVs etc. as they more and more come to realize how much those unnatural frequencies interfere with their increased brain function and frequencies.

Pay attention how often lights and electrical devices do malfunction or cease to function in your presence. Once your have realized how refreshing the absence of those 'stimuli' is, you discover how much you have yearned for your mind to focus on what is truly important in your life.

You further discover that your mind has been kept busy with much nonsense 'information' that is of no benefit to you. Most of the sound pollution keeps your mind in a dull state, not able to concentrate or think about your true needs, leaving you incapable to connect with your higher self.

The worst case finding and discoveries will be, that it becomes very obvious how much and to what high degree human minds have been unconsciously manipulated. One by one, humans of the Light are waking up to their true nature, capacities and meaning of life – once the mind manipulative machinery exits their lives. The awakened Light Beings will deconstruct old believe systems that kept them asleep and in illusion.

Understand that ascension means awakening to your true divine self.

Be aware that the dark forces will try to keep and lure you back into their web of misinformation and mind intruding control frequencies. Be prepared and know how to protect yourselves against nightly frequency intrusion, disturbing your restful sleep and hindering your brains full functioning. Be aware that the dark forces will feed you false information.

Be aware that depending on how much of this false information you let occupy your mind, it undoubtedly will influence your judgment about things, situations and other people.

Be aware that the dark forces will try to feed you fear. Know and understand to not let this enter and occupy your mind, reflect these thought patterns lovingly back to it's originators.

Have you never wondered how and why you made decisions you never thought you would?
Much mind manipulation is planned out in great detail and builds up over time. No human mind would ever knowingly enter into a destructive situation, where the chances of getting hurt or killed are greater than staying unharmed.

Research the months and years prior to a Nations entering into war. Pay special attention to small details such as... who are the main characters adored in movies (what are the professions of the heroes?), what are their roles, their behavior, what themes did print media prefer to use for advertising? Once you look closer, you discover that hatred is nourished on the very subtle level. It crawls into the human sub consciousness where it is least expected. Every human, small or adult, is at free will exposing themselves to such mind manipulation. There are great psychological studies on this topic, which we encourage you, dear reader, to consult.

We re-enforce the need for attention. Pay attention to what you keep your attention focused on, as human's energy goes where the attention is, your life follows .

We greatly desire that the human spirit of Light transforms the information business in such a way that it is used to form positive, enriching and nourishing thought patterns and no longer negative, harsh and soul harming. It is important for you to understand that the dark forces are living from all the negative thought frequencies. They feed off them. Once we stop having such negative thoughts in our lives, the dark will starve out.

ABOUT BEING HUMAN

Humans narcotize their senses in an unhealthy way. Their ears shall hear but they numb them with noise so loud and shrill making their souls cry. They do this so much until their inner wisdom starts to shut down in order to survive. Deaf they finally start to listen again. To listen to what is beneficial for them. Their deafness turns their hearing sense inward. Instead of hearing the leaves chatter in the trees or the breath of ocean waves, they hear their own blood stream and the rythmic beating of their heart.

Too many can not cope with the intensity with which their senses get overpowered. Their only escape is the inward refuge. How much richer are those, who choose consciously to use their freedom of choice to not expose their senses. Isn't it wonderful ? It is the endless freedom of choice we have on this planet. We are the ones who may choose who, what and how much is entering through our senses.

We can get carried away in the sounds of nature and those of other nature species and energies, which add to our experiences of the wonders and make us happy. This is one of the reasons of our being here. We also have the choice to narcotize our senses, all the way to harmful experiences. It is our choice to decide. Singing of birds, laughter, buzzing of insects, or deafness through loud screaming engines and aggressive yelling of dark Beings.

Color of flowers, crystals, stones, the oceans and the rainbows, or darkness. Touching in lust and gentle caressing, or cold, crippled nerve endings that hardly can tell the difference between cold and warm.

Delicate aromas while eating, or overpowered senses from chemical unnatural mixtures, which like acid, rob you of your finer taste sense.

Let us live with all our senses. They exist to enjoy them, as they provide you joy and happiness. Feel the sun on your skin. Smell the scent of the roses, lilac, iris... drink the aromas of the overwhelmingly rich world of herbs; listen to the songs of the birds, murmuring of a brook, mumbling of a spring in the woods; feel the velvety texture of soft fur when caressing an animal… dive into the rich blues and greens of the ocean, become One with the sound of the waves….
Get drunken by the colors of the flowers and the rainbow. Feel the sand under your feet.

Mother Earth wants you to be happy. It is your undeniable birthright, to be happy on this planet. It is your right to take in with all your senses the treasures of Mother Earth. So long until you feel the finest nuances with every sense…. So delicately that it can not be described in words, as the humanly sounds do not provide vowels, no imagery is fine enough to show, no music deeply sweet enough to resonate this beauty.

When you have reached this state, your senses have opened for the true experience of God.

You vibrate in harmony with all God-essence frequencies. You feel One with all being. You don't analyze the impressions of your senses, emotions, and feelings any longer. You just ARE.

You are one with the Earth, all energies, and you feel the feelings of other energy Beings, also those of the plants, flowers and animals. You feel how it is to be the air, being compressed and carrying sound waves. You feel how one note, like a stone dropped into water, ripples waves into all directions. You feel how noise impacts your own vibrations and how it causes turmoil deep inside.

To provide you an image of what happens inside you through sound, take a big bowl filled with water. Place it in front of you. Now bang the bowl in slow rhythm with a big spoon. Watch how and what waves are forming, and how they move. Now increase the speed of rhythm. Watch how the waves are changing. Finally bang fast <u>without</u> any rhythm …. Watch what happens to the water. Your body consists of 80% water and follows the same physical laws. However this will change, as humans will transform from a water based body to an energy based body.

Now you see why you do not feel well when you expose yourself to noise. You can feel how noise diffuses your frequencies, and bring you into dis-harmony with worse effect than any thunder could ever have. You feel the ocean waves, the breath of Mother Earth. Your etheric body provides so much more sensation than you know.

HOW TO BE CALM

Dearest daughter we have come together tonight to share with you the secret of being calm. Calmness and stillness of the mind are a major secret for enlightenment. Like the ocean always creates waves that splash at the shores, your mind continuously has waves of information flowing back and forth. Your mind could hardly be still, you say. Each one of you has their means to find calmness and stillness within your mind. You wonder how to find it? Each of you is unique, such is the way to stillness within your mind.

We ask you to remember that FEELING is the way to find YOUR stillness of mind. It takes practice to master FEELING. The senses which you have on this planet are to experience vibrations not through pure frequency but narrowed down as sound, colors, touch and smell. In order for you to be able to collect these experiences separately, the frequencies of vibration had to be lowered to third dimension density.

The senses you experience in Third Dimension are not the same senses your higher energy selves experience. In this realm you ARE pure energy, thus you do not have outside sensors to experience, because you are within and outside at the same time – as pure energy.

AS PURE ENERGY -

You experience the sweet scent of a flower AND you are the scent, at the same time.

You experience sound and you are the sound waves in the air. You feel the touch and are touch. You see the rainbow and you are the rainbow. It is a closed vibrational endless ellipse. You are here in one place receiving the vibration, and you are at the same time out there being the vibration. The closest you come to this oneness in a human incarnation is through being united with another human in true love - when you are in one another, feeling this total oneness with each other and everything.

ALL senses share one key element – FEELING.

FEEL the loving warmth of a beautiful flower scent – how does it make you feel?
FEEL the depth, richness and intensity of the rainbow colors – how does it make you feel?
FEEL the gentle, warm, softness of a touch – how does it make you feel?

Your feelings are happiness, love, feeling whole/complete, feeling safe and protected. Stay in these FEELINGS – in your mind – and experience stillness of mind.

The more you practice intentional FEELING, by recalling your emotions connected, the easier you will be able to still your mind.

Since FEELING is very unique to each of you, there is no recipe or standard tool/s to use. Be your teacher and student in this.

Find your way to BE! in the FEELING.
Teach yourselves to allow to FEEL
and notice how you change
to the essence of BEING.

FEEL that you ARE   and
BE! the FEELING.

LOVE EACH OTHER
AS YOU LOVE THYSELF

We once came forward with: "love each other as you love thyself". But how can today's Earth population love each other gently, when they don't know anymore how to love themselves?

Look around you, people of Earth. Who of you is honoring themselves? Why are you rushing and running through your days, year after year, and before you realize why you are on this planet, you used up your given time in doing useless things that did not assist your spiritual growth.

Turn around people incarnated on free-will-zone planet Earth! Look around you! What has been done to this planet that was entrusted to you for taking care of it? Everything needed to thrive spiritually has been provided but was neglected and in many cases even worse - destroyed. Consciousness has set in some time ago and subconsciously many of you KNOW what to do to assist and help GAIA – Mother Earth. Beware not to overdo it in the opposite direction now – as you are at the brink of time to tyranny under the cloak of "good will".

Your wish to incarnate on this planet at this time manifested, as you are the ones that can fulfill the mission. You are the most powerful Beings in the universe. KNOW THAT! Else you would not be here at this time.

Rest and take a break from rushing through your days.
Stop and take a look around you.
How far have you distanced yourself from contact with
Mother Earth and the nature
she provides so generously?

Step outside and breath!
Breath in the air.
Breath in the scents of flowers and herbs.
Breath in the Light!
Breath in Life!

Open up that shell you have created around you
for protection against true feelings and emotions
expressed by others and yourself.

Time is here to allow.
Allow to love yourself.
Allow others to love you.
Allow yourself to love others.
Allow yourself to feel whole and protected
in nature.

Call in the protecting light.
Surround yourself with it.

Work with it in your quite times dedicated to
meditation and prayers. Set aside times each day to
focus on your spiritual growth.

KNOW that you will be provided for.

The more you experience yourself in the Light, the more you will attract like Beings into your life. Experience the joy and happiness Light Beings bring. Be one with them.

KNOW that once you have made that last step into the Light, darkness can no longer reach you.

Many of you fear this last step. They know, once it's taken there will be no turning back. It means to leave the known comfort zone of existence and switching into conscious life.

Those who have struggled a long time before taking this last step into the Light, finally laugh at their own fears. They wonder why they indulged in misery and pain for so long.

You have incarnated to experience the full range of emotions and feelings. You incarnated many life times to do just that. Some of you are even edicted to the pain and convinced themselves that it is their only way to experience pleasure.

Feel into your own hearts, people of this planet. Each one of you is unique, down to your past life experiences, which you shall soon consciously remember to bring forth, your true Light and wisdom for the better of all.

SOUND LIGHT
BE!

Breath in the Light, Beings incarnated on Earth!

Sing celestial sounds so your soul remembers source.

BE! The true YOU that you are.

Remember where you come from.
All of you now incarnated, have lived life's
in Mu and Atlantis.
You all have Orion and Pleyadian energy.

KNOW
You are the ones your have been waiting for.

People of Earth your prayers have been heard!
The Gods and Being you have been asking for,
walk among you.

Just open your hearts and open your third eye….
And your soul and true self will recognize
the angels in your midst.

Ride the waves of true joy.

Be your inner child, as that is what was meant by
"let the children come to me". Come home into your
true self, through being your true pure childlike
innocent YOU.

Be the Light you are.
Be innocent as newly incarnated energies.

Look around you in wonder and stop analyzing beauty
and life to death. Take in the energies emitted by
nature and those enlightened Beings called angels.

Nourish your inner most.
Nourish your hearts with their presence.
Experience the joy their pure existence
brings into your life.

For some of you the experience of one
encounter with these Beings is enough to draw from
your entire life time. Imagine the joy and energy you
can have in meeting and experiencing many of these
Beings continuously. For your human body, not to
explode from sheer joy, love and energy – we ask you
to prepare for this experience in meditation. Regular
meditation raises your frequency. Meditation helps
your human body to raise beyond its present density of
Third dimensional existence.

True BEING in the Fifth Dimension will be
much different. Be prepared to know the thoughts of
other energies. Be prepared to read in their hearts.
Do not fear! As there will be no evil energies, those can
not pass into Fifth Dimension. Those Beings will
remain in Third Dimension density until they are ready
and evolved enough.
This is what is said to be Judgment Day.

Those of the Light and true heart shall raise with their bodies into Fifth Dimension, eternal Light, where there will be no more darkness. The others will remain in the "dark", blinded by the Light you emit when raising into Fifth Dimension. You will disappear and raise into the heavens for them.

YOUR SPECTRUM COLOURS

It is said that God shall come in a Rainbow. Those of you with eyes to see, have seen the rainbow colors in the skies and around the moon. It appears like another type of atmosphere building and growing around both planets.

Crystals have been awaking since a long time and they form a safe bubble around Mother Earth and the Moon. Since a long time the number of colors that human incarnations can see with their physical eyes have increased. Humans used to see only five colors in a rainbow: blue, green, yellow, orange and red. Now you see in addition: purple, magenta, dark red, light green and turquoise. You shall discover many more, which you will give new names.

One day soon your scientists will discover the true capabilities of crystals. All of you beings contain massive amounts of tiny crystals in liquid form. It is those crystals and the water flowing between, or better said carrying them, that allows communication of information from across the universe over great distance. It allows for your connection with source.

It is this pulsing flow of the universal energy that creates your life energy.
You absorb it through your chakras like food from the heavens.

You are programmed by yourselves
and you will awaken according to your program.
Be the spirit YOU !

See through the illusions the dark forces are feeding you daily, every minute. Interference waves and patterns are being directed towards you to intrude your brain, to keep your thoughts busy with nonsense and unessential information.

The dark forces fear your true powers, once unleashed, and so they do everything to hinder you from staying focused and clear in your minds.

They know what you truly are capable of, and thus try everything in their power to hinder your energies from flowing freely and your awakening to full power of manifestation. As long as your minds are blocked by misinformation and kept busy with it – the dark is safe and thrives. Once you Light Beings refrain from the manipulation, you very soon discover your true powers. You rediscover WHO you truly are.

Remember Earth is a free-will-zone. You let the dark play you, because you are granting your permission for the experience. It is the law of the universe.

People of Earth wake up!
Wake up to your true power of Light and Love.
Wake up to your true hearts knowledge.
Wake up to the purity of your mind.
Wake up to see and understand.
Wake up to your true colors.
Wake up!
Deep inside of you, you know the truth.
You don't need anyone to tell you.
You KNOW it.
We are pointing merely the way.
The ones who can enlighten you – is YOU!
The ones to guide you – is YOU!
YOU!
All it takes is to wake up,
love yourself,
honor who you truly are,

BE!
And allow.
Allow the good to enter your life.
Allow the support and assistance
that is patiently waiting since a long long time.
Allow the Light Being to emerge, that you truly are.

BE!

AWAKENING II.

What we have come forth to tell is the essence
you need to awaken.
You awaken yourself.
You grant yourself to hear your wake up call!

We joyfully send the sounds of love from source
pulsing through the universe. You can receive it, once
you are tuned in – just like a radio that can receive a
multitude of waves at once but is ready to receive from
one station. It is YOU, in this free-will-zone, to choose
what signal you allow to receive. To demonstrate a
visual of what the "dark" does by sending subliminal
information your way….Consider yourself being like a
big crystal bowl filled with pure water. This body of
water inside your crystal self is pulsed by sound waves.
As long as these sound waves correspond with your
inner pulse, the body of water resonates in harmony.

Human that you are we encourage you to get a
visual of what was said. Take a big bowl, fill it with
water. Than bang the bowl in a harmonious slow
rhythm. Watch the wave pattern. Now switch to
disruptive arrhythmic discords and fast paced change in
rhythm. Watch the wave pattern ! THAT is what you
allow the "dark" to do to you! Your body consists of
80% liquid that reacts to sound waves *exactly* the same
way. In fact it is the easiest way and most powerful
tool to cause massive discomfort to large groups of
human beings at once.

And there is not much they can do to block the intrusion as sound waves are not only picked up by the human ear, but also by the entire water structure of the human body. The human body is like one large ear! Know that the human body will change from a water based body to an energy based body.

Sending unhearable ultra-sound waves in high frequency pulses towards a human being can be more effective than any gun could ever be. Such waves can knock a human out instantaneously, or worse....

We remind you of shattering glass by the sound of a soprano and during an Earthquake. Crystals contained in quartz sand, used in house construction, resonates with sound frequencies. Therefore sound can make buildings collapse and turn them into a listening device.

The opposite is true as well. Healing can be done much more efficient through harmonious sound waves, pulsing and massaging the inside water body of the human. KNOW what you allow being done to you. You are by nature whole, healthy and in balance with unlimited resources of energy. It is YOU who allow the discord.

Many of you have been "running" on discord for so long, that they consider this the normal state of being. You forgot what it feels like to be in harmony. In fact you feel discomfort when the discord is removed, so used are you to it. Just like the bowl filled with water, it takes calmness before the harmony waves can wash over your soul and harmony returns.

Be in harmony with your true self, and you will send out pulsing waves and Light that is received as healing and soothing by others.

It is this gentle harmony, which their subconscious recognizes. They immediately feel the longing to be in harmony. Listen to your own accord. Each one of you is linked through harmony. You pulse in frequency with Mother Earth.

You feel whole and good in structures whose measures translate into harmony. And you feel uncomfortable in structures of disharmony. (*I teach interior design and architecture applying ancient principals of sound. Ref. my book on this subject*)

It is sacred geometry that creates harmony.
It is sacred numerology that creates harmony.
And it is harmonious sound in the rhythm
of your heart beat
that brings you back into balance.

When we advise you to refrain from harsh environments, this includes sound. There are vehicles that roar and howl like screaming dragons described in ancient stories.

Feel into that sound next time you notice it. It shatters your harmony and brings you out of balance right down in your core, your solar plexus. How long do you want to tolerate such intrusion, disturbing your wellbeing?

Understand that such sounds can destroy you.

The crystal cities of Lemuria were destroyed through discord sound impulses. The walls of Jericho tumbled down through sound waves. Bridges collapse when an army marches in synchronized rhythm over it.

WAKE UP! And understand that no structure other than created from base elements will withstand a sound wave attack. Why do we still find stone pyramids? Not because the ancients were primitive. In fact they were much more advanced than people today. They knew that only base elements would survive frequency shifts. Thus they used base element stone and mind formed it to record information. Information in form of sacred geometry, numerology and astrology.

The interpretation of hieroglyphs was invented and is far from their true meaning. Wake up! The hieroglyphs are energy symbols, far reaching in their meaning on many layers, yet generously beautiful in their simplicity once your minds are able to grasp the aspects and layers of knowledge required to comprehend their full meaning.

Know that in Giza, Egypt are two more very large pyramids not visible to the human eye in Third Dimension. Those of you with eyes to see, can see them. These pyramids are of a different density and dimension. They hold technologies highly evolved. To avoid misuse of these technologies, these pyramids have been carefully hidden from the impure minds and "dark". Only the true hearted are able to see them.

HIEROGLYPHS II.

Dearest beloved Beings - gentle ones!
We come forward from your ancient future.
Resonate what we bring forth, in this time of birthing
your new bodies of conscious **ISNESS**.
Rejoice! You shall be new again!

ILLAH ILLAHMEH!

Guard your ways to the fulfilling Lights of truth.
Read the flashing pulsing Lights, take in their powers.
Feel the rotating beams of color we send you.
Embrace the vibrational scents,
riding the Lights of the skies.

Leave your limitations behind
and remember who you are.
Your capacities will show you the way.
Follow yourselves.
Follow no other, BUT yourselves.
you shall be free in the KNOW.

Begin to reflect and resonate with all.
All that is, all that was, all that will be.
It is time to be in your NOW.
Awaken gentle ones!
Awaken to your knowing.

Open your beautiful EYES,
all structures and beyond.
(chakras of the human, buildings Spaces and places)
SEE what you have always known
(they used the expression oughfnaa,
meaning more than only seeing with human eyes).
FEEL what you have always known.
(the sensory impression was feeling with my aura and body)
Ride the sound- and aroma-waves
of your home stars
and reopen the energy gates
leading your way home.

Sparkle – stars that you are.
Sparkle your eyes, to recognize each other *(aura).*
Blink your all encompassing energy solids
to travel home.
Your loving families await your powerful coming.
We feel with you from our higher dimensions
And wish we could be YOU

YOU are the chosen ones
Ascended already, returned by choice
For the highest good of all

Another voice comes in

Gentle ones! Go and understand the messages
you left yourselves. You have left them so beautifully
touching all senses, knowing how 'low density flesh'
would be curious to decipher the deeper layers of
meaning.

Remember, it is you, who left these messages behind. Uncover your secrets and use them to master the coming shifts. Third Dimension density caused blockages in your imagination of possibilities in different dimensions. Take the symbols, mirror, turn and spin them in the geometric solids. Break down the barriers of up and down, above / below, left and right THEN understand the beauty of it all.

Laugh, Beings of Light incarnated on Earth ! Your hearts will be so light and full of joy, once you comprehend the beauty of their meaning.

The pulsing of your laughter
will resonate in the entire universe.

LAUGH! GENTLE ONES!

SHINE YOUR LIGHT

Dearest we greet you from behind the veil. Things are getting clearer for all of you soon. They start happening already and shall be seen very soon on the Third Dimensional level. Know that you are carried by a huge support group all around the planet. Time has come for all of you to come forward. Your numbers are vast.

Rest assured that you shall be protected and taken care of. We are asking our Ambassador of Light to form support groups no larger than 12 people. These groups shall meet regularly to discuss their spiritual experiences. This shall reassure each one of you on your path and show yourself your spiritual development. When you discover that you are out-growing your group, let your intuition guide you to find another one, that suits your development level better. There is no being better than others or being slower. Each one of you shall open according to your divine plan in your own time. Do no longer judge yourselves based on others. You live your very own unique experiences, that are only for you.

Support groups shall form in which each one has a specific specialty to offer to the group, that none other can provide. You shall learn to experience the Fifth Dimension together. Think and feel as ONE Being, not as 12 separate Beings. Your experience of the Fifth Dimension will be a group experience. All of you will be carried by your group.

The group will be your chosen family. You will be free to move and change between groups anywhere on the planet.

You ask if these groups shall be mixed, male and female. We can not answer this for you. You yourselves will need to find out what suites your unique spirituality best. And since you develop, you will move on. All groups will be in change. We understand that the pure thought of mixed groups might cause distractions to some of you. Beloved let your spirit guides take the lead to 'your' group. Allow yourselves to feel what feels whole, healthy, good and makes you truly happy in your innermost.

You will discover that groups only stay and work together for certain periods. Within the group, single Beings will feel the urge to be alone, like hermits. This will happen to all of you. You will dedicate special 'alone time' for your spiritual growth. Be prepared for those moments and walk away to where you are guided to be for these times. In those times you shall go into deep meditations, clearing and cleansing, recharge your energies and rejuvenate.

We are tasking our Ambassador of Light to create and form monastery and convent like structures, where people can come to spend their alone time in a cell, without having to bother about material things such as food, water etc.. It will all be provided by the new society for you. As you shall return strengthened with new insights, society will benefit from you, feeding them back your increased wisdom.

To provide you in your present Third Dimension an understanding how this 'alone time' will be regarded - it shall be viewed like what you call *work* today. It will be the work on advancing yourself spiritually, from which ONENESS will gain.

Understand dearest ones that whatever each one of you learns, understands, gains insight in, will be known and understood by all of you. Your ONENESS means also ONE MIND with nearly unlimited potential.

We understand for some cultures on planet Earth this may sound scaringly familiar when looking back in time at old political systems. Rest assured, what is to come can not be compared in any way with those systems.

What is to come has nothing to do with political directions, ideology, systems, organizations...
All Beings of planet Earth will be connected and joined in ONENESS. There is no more separation, other than for the times spend in retreat alone. Now some of you will be reminded of disastrous mind control movies.

Those are the thoughts of the darkness, as that is what they have been practicing on you for a very long time. You just have not realized the truth.

Beloved see through the illusions of your 'reality'. The dark is holding you in their dense thought patterns, keeping you in constant fear and thus under control since a very long time.

The darks' greatest fear is that you, Beings of the Light, wake up to your true selves and realize the powers you own inside.

Beloved know that your future holds ONENESS. In that ONENESS mind control and fear will be unknown. Everyone is part of the loving whole. Only pure hearted Beings will make the transition into Fifth Dimension. Their thoughts, minds and hearts will be open books to everyone making this transition. Beings that want to hide aspects of themselves, will not be able to make this transition to the Fifth Dimension. They shall remain in Third Dimension until they are ready.

Great Beings and spirits such as St. Germain, have secured the worlds financial support long time ago for the time when your ascension comes. Rest assured that life will not be cumbersome in this realm. Know that you can manifest anything by thought instantaneously. As everyone will be able to create in such way, material competition - as existent today in your Third Dimensional world - will fall away.

As a Being of the Fifth Dimension your goals will be to further and grow spiritually even more. In the beginning you will be like small children. It will take time to get used to your experiences within the Fifth Dimension. Teleporting, transmitting a wealth of information and messages through pure thought, in the blink of a second, time which no longer will exist as you know it ...

People of Earth it will take an experimental while for you to get used to your new reality. That experimental period will be followed by a period of playfulness.

Then finally you will no longer be like little children in the new realm. You will start to use your new powers and technology for the furthering of ALL.

All Light Beings on this new planet and reality will be ONE mind, with an enormously large input of experiences and sensing all the time. You shall require more but much shorter rest times because of this.

The joining of pairs in true love will of course exist. Those pairs who choose to be together alone, will do so. But they will miss their group experiences and will join a new group together, after a while.

You may now ask about THE ONE MIND EXPERIENCES in this respect. Know that the joined love experiences will be the private experience of each one of you. Those feelings and emotions you shall only share, in the oneness of mind, heart, soul and spirit with your partner of true love. The group and others will not be able to tap into your privacy.

TURBULENCE
OF
FREQUENCY SHIFTS

PHYSICAL AND EMOTIONAL TURBULENCES

Dear people of Earth, do not get disrupted by the sound the final uproar of the dark will create in a huge final disaster. Sound is vibration. You are of vibration. Frequency vibrates. Any sound outside your own bodily harmony frequency triggers fear. Sound causes vibrations inside your human dense bodies and can create disharmony. Sound waves can destroy much of that which is. And the dark shall attempt to use it for their purpose.

Know, beings of light, that the vibrations of your frequency are much higher, and it is only in the human bodies through which you can be reached by the lower frequencies. It is their gate to enter the light bodies. It is part of your free will experience of this incarnation. You have asked for this lesson before you came. This is what you wanted to experience.

Many Beings throughout the universe look upon you. Many wanted to be here at this time to experience what you experience. Through this experience, and in overcoming the vibrations of fear, you will propel yourselves into the next dimension. It will be such a boost. Many Beings throughout this and other galaxies are eager to hear you teach of your experiences.

You shall then see (*they used the term* oughefnaa *which includes many more senses than what a human can comprehend as seeing, so they only describe what will be visible*) that the lower half of your bodily structure is semi translucent and you are emitting energy in Light form.

MIND CONTROL AND MANIPULATION

The dark has been bombarding your homes, schools, work places, public places… everywhere you go with subliminal messages and sound frequencies to disturb your minds from being clear. There is hardly any place without these mind intruding frequencies from the dark.

The majority of mankind has stopped reflecting on information they are fed. You eagerly buy gossip and misinformation. With a clear mind you would recognize the misinformation and lies. The dark is using their satellite technology to bombard your brains with frequency to prevent and hinder you from understanding who you truly are. They have no interest in you waking up to your full powers – as the Light Being that you are is extremely powerful. When your frequencies and minds are numbed by thousands of useless, meaningless information impulses every day, you are easier to control. The dark is and has been conditioning you this way, for whatever they need your consent on.

They intrude your sleep at night by shooting down signals. They have you go into fear over nothing. You are so easy to manipulate in your low human frequency.

Once you wake up to your spirituality and be the Light Being you are, these lower frequencies can not reach you any longer. We understand that it is difficult to break these chains of mind control imprisonment. Stop believing what you are fed.

Wake up to your own true self. What you feel to be true is what IS true. We ask you to question what you are shown and told. Question the sources, who they are, on who's paymaster list they are.

Awake yourself! **BE!**

Be the light that you truly are.

THE MINDLESS

Aside the final big sound attack by the dark, there will be the *mindless*. They will run around and stir up your communities and families. Feeding false information. Causing much discussions occupying your minds with mindless thoughts of total irrelevance.

They are doubters of their self, easy prey of the dark. They follow blind. Their minds are split. They can not reconcile their sensory impressions with what they were taught to believe through various belief systems (*governments, religions, communities, social groups* ....).

A major collapse of belief systems called *religions* goes hand in hand with the final uproars of the dark and the following collapse of governments. Those changes will be even more shaking to all population than the events in nature. This will weaken the majority of Earths population, since they will be robbed of the only faith they had and kept holding on to in this existence.

These Beings will be in total shock and may decide to leave the planet. The dark will use this scenario to gather many forces behind them and by creating false beliefs, which the weak will follow blindly. The dark will create holographic imagery across the world to cause fear. It anables them to force people to follow the darks' belief systems, which they will feed.

It will be then, when the Light shall set you free. Feel into what is shown to you. If it feels fake, it IS fake. Trust your intuition and feelings more than your eyesight (*here they mean the human eyes*).

Those in doubt, unable to reconcile what they see, what they feel and what they know, have chosen this lesson. They become the mindless. They become the final tools of the dark. They will scream and yell to cover up their own despair and fears. They will try to force new beliefs unto you. Leave them to it. It is the fear of the mindless, working for the dark, guiding them. The dark calculated them into their equation. Leave them to their own low resonating frequencies. Part from them.

People of Earth understand that this may happen in your smallest groups called family. Understand that each Being of a family may have come here for another purpose during this great time of change, and that your purpose may not be theirs.

This may be hard and it is the only part – the human emotions - we could not test on our higher plains, but we know that many of you already have understood this and taken steps to let go of these Beings, to allow them their experiences they came in for.

Find the Light Beings in your area, wherever you go. Stay with them. They are your true family. You will recognize and find each other.

You will understand that each one of you Light Beings is so much stronger than you can presently comprehend. You would not be in this incarnation, if you were not among the strongest energetic Beings in this universe.

YOU ARE THE MOST POWERFUL ENERGIES IN THIS UNIVERSE.

We want you to become clear about the fact that the emotional and physical disruptions will go hand in hand in your human experience. You knew this, when you choose this exciting time for being here and to help with the transition.

You know that your higher Light frequency can create sounds that will 'wash away' the dark. Many of you had visions of this scenario. *How this will come about is outlined in a separate book.* Sound is so much stronger and more powerful than anything your human mind knows. Sound can shatter lower frequencies called matter. It can ex- & implode structures of low frequency, called matter, with the effects of an invisible bomb.

There are frequencies in ranges not noticeable to the human ear. The dark has used such unhearable sound attacks but you have failed to understand them as such. You let your human eyes get betrayed in massive illusions created by the dark. Their methods of misinformation, distracting and occupying your minds with visible actions on matter, to distract you from noticing the obvious, has served the dark for a very long time. It is time to awaken your senses!

Look the opposite direction, when the dark is pulling your attention in one way, and see what really is Happening, that they don't want you to see. It has been hiding in plain view – your minds have just been pulled into another direction.

The dark has played and toyed around with your limited human senses. Refuse to play their game. Deny them access to your brains through your human senses. They have been abusing frequencies far too long.

Know that you, Beings of the Light, are much stronger than they want you to know. We have been raising Earth frequencies to awaken your extensive senses from off world, one by one, gently. You know that you can block the darks' mind intrusions. You consciously can prevent from being toyed with.

Begin using your spiritual level powers. This is how you draw from the increasing Earth frequencies, to strengthen and awaken your additional senses. Only through strengthening your spirit you will be able to prevent damage to your bodily matter, which is vibrating in the lower frequencies. As long as you vibrate in the lower frequencies your body will stay matter.

Healers we call upon you. Come forth now to share your wisdom of energy healing. Rebalance the lower matter by infusing them with pure energy of the light to ease their transition. Heal them so they can be strong to progress on their way to enlightenment.

This is the grand World healing you have always known to be here for.

WE want you to understand that the term ENLIGHTENMENT is to be taken literally in the upcoming turbulences. Those of the Light shall shine. All evolving shall see and emit this Light. Know that your vibrational levels are much higher than those of the dark. You are out of their reach. They can not reach you, although they may try. But again it is the law of frequency that the higher can look into the lower but not the opposite. Understand that you shall then become totally invisible to the dark. For them you will simply disappear, dissolve. Many of you Light Beings have already experienced this.

You approached people and they did not see you – they are of the dark. You started talking or asking someone – they could not hear you – they are of the dark. Beings of the Light know that this will now be your daily usual encounters. It will be so easy for you to tell the dark from the Light Beings.
Enjoy the simplicity and beauty it.

Light Beings you know that you are the ones leading the way for Mother Earth, to come through her frequency shifts and turbulences, as a cleansed sparkling beauty. The New Golden Age is dawning. Send your healing powers and energies around Mother Earth. Provide a cocoon of loving energy for her Light to shine.

The more you feed Mother Earth with your loving energy, the easier she will be able to go through the transformation in frequencies. You hold her, you help birthing her new frequency. The mineral Beings have already established an outer shell around Mother Earth to protect her from the photon storms and to ease her being steered into another area in this universe. Earth will become your spaceship to steer into Sirius dominion where the two suns will shine.

Light Beings unite.
BE! the strength you are!
BE! the power you are!
BE! the love you are!

You are almighty when you stand in your Light.
It is YOUR time NOW.
Stand up!
Stand together!
Focus and gather your energy and you will know…
You are one with source.
You ARE source.
BE!

SCIENCE

We are coming forth to talk about science of the future. There will be new fields of science of the human Light Beings. Being of most part pure energy based bodies you will be able to do research in areas so far closed for you.

SPACE, DISTANCE AND TIME

It will be discovered that the void is not empty but filled with energy Beings. If these energies would not fill this space, space would collapse.

When a major volume of energies consciously decides to leave a given volume of space, space folds and collapses. Once it will be understood that space in the universe is filled with energies of certain dimensions and property, this will become clearer.

Based on possible communication with these space occupying energies, agreements can be arranged that lets other energies pass space without much effect of distance and time, which are invented thought models for alternate realities to share space. In other words, any space is occupied by energies of various properties and frequencies. The energies themselves share the same source. So they exist in multiple realities which can be nearly identical, experiencing different scenarios, patterns and options.

Time is a thought model to allow simultaneous experience in many realities. For example, energies in human bodies of Third Dimension slip during their sleep time into these other realities and experience "time" there. Once it has become clear that you as the energy co-exist in simultaneous versions, dreams will be evaluated new.

As a Third dimensional human Being you will no longer wonder where all the pain and bruises come from over night. You will know they originated from your energetic experience in another reality of your existence.

The veils, so many have been talking about in your Third Dimension, are these co-existing realities. In gaining new possibilities in the next dimension, you can willing- and consciously switch into these realities with ease.

Time exists parallel. Present, past and future exist next to each other, not after each other. Only in parallel time, energies can move freely between realities.

Imagine a ribbon of one yard length. One end is the past, the middle is the present and the other end is the future. The ribbon is of the same material regardless of past, present or future. Now bring both ends together, so the ribbon forms an endless ring or loop. That is your time line. EVERYTHING EXISTS AT ONCE AND ONLY THE DISTANCE BETWEEN THEM GIVES THE ILLUSION OF TIME.

Now create smaller and smaller loops with this endless connected ribbon. You are folding time and space. The smaller the loops the closer get past, present and future. You can make the loops so small, that all time and space exists together in one tiny particle. In other words, you have folded time and space into one defined millisecond nucleus of an atom.

Here is where you discover the smallest particle of being – it is intangible thought. It does not exist of matter, so it can not be influenced nor measured by matter. It can however be influenced by thought and reacts instantaneously to thought patterns.

IT IS AWARE OF ITS OWN EXISTENCE.
IT CREATES.
IT IS THE ESSENCE OF BEING.

SCIENTIFIC RESEARCH IN YOUR NEXT DIMENSION
will be on

- Mutative Morphosis
- Comparable Transgression
- Wave functions of realities
- Space stretching
- Vortex gravities
- Densities of solid gases
- Sound transportation
- Information Technology of Crystals
- Liquid Crystal Transducers
- Machicolative transcendence
- Correlation of co-existing multiple space-time continuums
- Navigation of crystal structures

Some of these research projects you will master in other dimensions. Various of your scientists will leave their physicality at will, to complete their research in new incarnations of another dimension.

Understand that many of the Beings incarnated now for the time of shift into higher dimension, are among the most brilliant scientists and leaders of the universe. They have ascended to much higher dimensions and have chosen to help and assist you and Mother Earth in your growth process and ascension. They are here to ensure your transition will be as smooth as possible. They will steer space ship Earth, with you, gently to its new location.

MEDICINE

In the medical field common knowledge and use of energy clearings, vibratory sound and light treatments will be practiced by everyone. These types of treatments will additionally function as frequent retreats, available in special dedicated spaces inside the living space.

Special areas very clear and clean with certain Earth energies will be used to grow herbs and flowers for medical purposes. Aromatherapy will be daily part of nourishment. Overall Beings will much more focus on their health – physical and mental health.
With their energies being of a much higher frequency the importance of relaxation and staying centered will be realized. Since Beings will run on high level frequency pulsation in exchanging and retrieving information and communication they will need to relax for specific periods of time.

The absence of mind pressing and stress creating issues like "having to find a job, or housing, need to make money" will result in great sadness and a feeling of emptiness which requires treatment. Therapists will form groups to heal these suffering from such post Third Dimensional depressions and traumata. Also the absence of competition (as everyone can create by thought the need for competition eliminates itself) will cause in some Beings traumatic experiences unknown today.

Entire professions will break away, as they become obsolete such as doctors, nurses, bankers, politicians (governments), the entire news sector (TV, Radio, newspapers). As all Beings can plug into the overall awareness, everyone will just know.

The highest goal for all will be to learn and increase knowledge, to share with all.
The other high esteemed goal will be relaxation and cleansing of the mind, to stay as pure as possible.

LIVING

Living will be in groups of 12 – where each Being has its specific function and duties, complementing its own area of expertise and what each Being loves to do – will be common. There will be no low key duties. Everything is valued evenly important and is understood as an essential part for the functioning of the entire group.

Members of these groups are free to change into another group. All are free to move to other locations and parts of the world. Since each Being fully understands the value it has to the functioning of the entire group, changes into new groups will be done very responsible.

Before this new group living concept eliminates cities and villages known today, the new mankind will go through some adjusting phase. This phase will not take very long, as the overall consciousness comprehends very fast the benefits of such smaller groups. The groups will form based on interest and age. In other words, there will be groups who focus on research of certain subjects, and only stay together for the duration of the research project. This can be years or only weeks.

There will be groups with focus on healing areas in other parts of the universe. Groups specializing in communication with the dolphins, whales and other species.

To give you sort of a comparison to your Third Dimensional understanding – instead of going to a seminar or being an employee of a company you freely select a group to live with, until you feel you have learned enough on the subject – and then you move on.

Always keep in mind
that the highest goal of source
is to learn and understand more.

RELAX – IT is LAW

As all Beings are constantly interacting with each other on various levels, there will be a great need for retreats and time spend alone.

To ensure that everyone takes these needed breaks, it will be a law to go to a retreat frequently. To keep the mind clear and focused will be one of the main health factors for all. People will spend long times in such retreats to get centered again. To be in the Self.

During such retreats people will also be shown new areas to research and learn, to avoid one sided focus. Therapists will assist you to clear yourself.

Let us remind you – you will have full resemblance of all your past life experiences and knowledge collected. It will take a lot of energy to maintain this in your consciousness on all levels of your being. We mean all emotions you ever felt, all experiences ever made will be fully remembered! Clearing and relaxing will be very desired by you. Going to the retreat will be valued like your present Third Dimensional vacation bonus and all holidays together at once.

TEACHINGS AND PREPARATIONS
FOR ONENESS

Dearest we are coming forth with additional information. Tonight we are coming forth with more scientific data which we ask you to pass on. This once again is information for scientists of the very near future.

The new and higher energy frequencies that your world is now beginning to experience will establish the basis for the technologies that our space brothers are holding for you. We realize that you will go through serious bodily changes that will not be easy for most of you to adjust to in the short period of time.

We encourage you to spend much time outdoors with bare feet on Mother Earth so you are able to connect through your foot chakras with the new frequencies that Mother Earth is now holding. This will enable you to adjust easier and faster to the new systems we are about to put in place.

Many of you have now realized that the systems in place religious, economically and financially are falling apart. It is now up to you to define where you want to take the future of this planet. You have decided to incarnate for this important time on this planet, it is your reason for being here now.

We hand you, together with the new frequencies, also the memories to all your past lifetime wisdom from the ancients and from all your off planet experiences, being one with your brethren. It is time to remember, thinking of all your minds as one.

You are all interconnected. The time has come to remember that you all are one Being. You together have a wisdom and knowledge far more sophisticated than any of your computer technologies in place. You are magnificent creators, almighty in your power.

It is time to remember this knowledge, once you have cleansed your mind completely. Then you will be able to reconnect with each other.
Once you learn and understand (remember) to tab into each others reference libraries, stored in your mental memory banks/ links on subatomic levels, you will be able to accomplish and manifest everything with greatest ease instantly.

Once you have reached this level of consciousness, you will be able to do anything you wish with this beautiful planet Earth, that is yours. You will be able to fly it, wherever you want to go, by pure thought.

We realize that thinking as One Being will take experience and re-learning. We therefore are forcing you to gather in groups to exchange your knowledge and experiences, on how to use your mental capacities.

Additionally you will experience the power you truly have, as you will create willingly new scenarios. Understand that your brain waves are not only created by your brain. Understand that you have thought forms and patterns throughout your human bodily structure.

Your scientists have always wanted to find the smallest particle of existence. They discovered the nucleus of atoms and went further to the tiniest photon level... yet they still have not found the smallest particle there is...

They will soon discover that the smallest particle is a thought form, highly capable of manifesting at will. This will be extremely difficult to comprehend for studied, preset mindsets.

Non-scientists, with an open mind, will comprehend these findings easier, as their minds are not blocked with models and theories of how things should work. Your scientists will have to open up their minds much further, to allow a total new way of thinking, else they will not understand how matter is composed through manifestation.

All matter on planet Earth is a living thought form in existence through will. Entire planet Earth is a free will zone. Therefore the most magnificent thought forms exist here to experience life form from different perspectives – inside, outside and around the planet.

Dearest we know you feel like you have read all this before. Be assured you have not. This is coming through form us, but because you are a highly evolved Being and scientist of the finest off-world places, you do know a great deal of all that we are bringing forth. Please have patience in the process. It is the reason we have send you with all your scientist background from your work with Metatron, so that you are able to answer any additional questions that will / may come up in the future. So we ask you to stay open to receive the data we are sending. Rest assured that you will be able to answer instantaneously questions addressed to you from highly accomplished scientists.

With the increase in frequency you will be able to see many more thought forms around your world. The void that human have thought they see, is in fact filled with other thought forms that co-exist with all of the others.

The air is filled with thought forms of another energy frequency. The same holds true for the universe. The space you consider empty and black is indeed filled with flowing and pulsing energies, which transport thoughts, thought forms and information between dimensions, you don't even know yet exist.

Soon you start to understand that your created human sound language will not be sufficient to transport the full understanding of what will be your new experience. It will be then, that you will understand the true meanings of the symbolic ancient languages.

At the same time, all will come to realize, that what you call 'ancient' is in fact your future, to which you finally are reconnecting.

Numerous realities co-exist within each other, in the 'space' of planet Earth. Several of them will collapse into one another, at a time in the near future. This is what we need to get you ready for. It will be strange to see yourself in a number of realities at once, and folding these realities together into one energy existence that you truly are.

We will ensure, that you will not face an over-load of information at once. It is our plan to make this as easy on you as possible. We therefore will not allow more than three realities to show up at once. Once you have mastered those, the next set will enter. This is what you will experience as further ascensions or initiations.

Many of you are not yet awake and have no understanding of their true identities. We understand that this can be a shock for those. Here again we are trying to make it easy on you. We could test and mathematically calculate how biological matter will react within your human bodies, but what we have been unable to calculate are your emotional patterns. Those are left untouched in the free will zone of planet Earth. The emotional transitions will be the most difficult for you, while progressing through the dimensional frequency shifts. This is one very important reason for forming groups to exchange your experiences on all levels.

It will form a bond of understanding and support, needed for what is to come. You will need to be able to fully trust each other, on all levels, in order to make the ascension into Fifth Dimension.

To support the teachers we have instructed this highly evolved being – Ambassador of Light - whom we are coming forth through- to share all information provided to her over the last two decades. The methods we have provided her with for herself, will also benefit many others. We recently came through with meditation and prayer assistance, that will assist you in staying aligned and centered through all the upheaval heading towards you.

In order to be stable as guides, leaders and teachers for all the others, who will not be as ready for what is coming, you will yourself need help. And the teachings of meditations and prayers we have given to this entity, will assist you in staying focused, centered and connected.

WE are all one.
Together we can reach the highest heights of wisdom.

TOUCHED BY THE
MOUNTAIN CRYSTAL

We are growing in number right now.
We will be found soon.
We are here to assist you in accomplishing your goals.
We must not be moved from our present location,
as it would cause imbalance.

Ensure that the obelisks in Egypt are put back into
place. No, it need not be the originals. We know that
would be impossible due to States pride. A crystal of
same shape, 2/3 the height, would be best to place
instead.
See whichever you can initiate in statesmen brains.
For planetary healing it is essential to start this.

Singing in front of the Lion clawed head is
essential. It will start the resonators in crystalized form
inside, which start connecting with the higher realms
surrounding this planet and deep down inside. Be the
one to start this.

ON BODY

The following channeled information is personal. It contains information which I consider valuable to others.
So I am sharing it.

Why does love also involve feeling hurt?
It is all part of your learning in this incarnation. In order for you to understand what you have and are giving to others, you need to know what it feels like – this is not just for you, it is for you to understand how you make others feel.

You mean I make others feel hurt? I am not aware of ever having done that, at least not intentionally. If I did I regret this very much.
Please stop being so hard on yourself! No, you did not hurt others and their feelings. You are not capable to do so. The most you ever can cause in another human being is sort of disappointment. But no more than that. You are a walking living angel. You are a mirror to other Beings, in which they see what they can be. You are not aware of it, but you initiate A LOT of change in the life's of every human you meet. They see who you are. They see your crystal filled aura. Only you do not see, who you truly are as else you could be overwhelmed. One day you will grasp the full impact you had to this world and time – but that will be the time when you are leaving. Stop trying to understand this part of your being here.

Stop searching for this truth, as it will only be revealed
when you have chosen to leave this incarnation.
We compliment you, on how fast and thorough you
healed and maintain it. You now understand that
thought is cause. All we think manifests and you are
doing absolutely wonderful in holding your thoughts
focused on the goals and thus are seeing results.
Keep doing your morning and evening exercises as it
helps you staying grounded. It eases moving around
between the realms, which you do so much.

LEARNING TO BE!

OUR (SOURCE) DESIRE IS LEARNING. You, who you are of the higher frequencies, have always felt the yearning to learn new things. Learning all possible experiences in a human body on planet Earth. You have reached all there is to experience, on this level of existence. We have learned through you.

In the process you nearly destroyed yourselves. You imposed barriers on yourselves and gained strength in breaking them down again. Your biggest enemy has been fear, which you overcame victoriously. The grandest obstacles we watched you create inside your minds, on emotional levels. We observed and felt with you. You have overcome your separation from source and are now approaching ONENESS.

TIME HAS COME TO BE NEW — TO BE YOU. By transforming yourselves, you are born again into who you truly are. With approaching Fifth Dimension fast, you shall become co-creators and live in expanded ways. Instant healings and manifestations are then possible through the awakening of your full DNA codes. Many of you have already seen visuals of these code downloads at night (like crop-circles for Mother Earth, and symbols from ET for the combined beings). You shall experience mind to mind communication and wonder about your former ways.

All will be healers, understanding the elements of healing: Intention, imagination and love.

Use the Egyptian wheels to travel together, to meet and consult with other energies. Lay down on the ground forming a circle, feet meeting in the center. Then go into guided meditation using crystals.

Through reverse gravity you shall make vehicles fly and hover with ease.

Through temperature balancing you will strengthen underwater structures.

You communicate knowledge on many levels, including connected emotions through slipping into each others thoughts. You exchange information by standing around crystal surfaces which you touch with thought and images will be shown to all surrounding.

You shall discover the limitations of your present sound language, and discover so many more layers of communication, including sound, light, color, image in a multitude of dimensions. The new communication is poetry of mind, spirit and color.

Beings of Earth, you, the ones who are going through the dimensional shifts. Know there are many Beings from far away galaxies, awaiting eagerly your teachings. You are the great teachers and like all great teachers, you have been great students. You are the chosen ones. The strongest in all the universe, who came to help Mother Earth go through the shifts and birth herself new into the Golden Age.

This page intentionally left blank

FINAL WORDS

Dearest Beloved, keep your attention focused
on your goals.
Call upon us – your guides and angels.
We see and understand your pressing needs.
Trust that we are working on creating the
circumstances needed and sending the appropriate
help, people, sources
and resources your way.
All you need to do is to allow them to enter your life.
Lean back and expect to receive.
Do not worry nor fear.
You are safe and protected wherever you are.
Do not worry about your loved ones.
They fulfill their own chosen path,
which we ask you to respect.

BE! ready for the changes.
UP is your way together.
You are here for something GRAND.

We thank you for being our channel
through which we are going to teach the future
leaders.
We take our leave now.
Blessings and love to all !

LIGHT LANGUAGE

Ishataya ijatya
Illa illameh, illa illamuh

Santonam hibu set ante igula hasinat em
Washanaja isat julom
Istjanium estene halojatiah

Ishana katawah esinet
Eli hudujah esinet havet

Illalah illah eshatam

Salutat!

CLOSING WORDS

I thank all the energies and Beings – the Ashantara - who have chosen me to serve as Ambassador of Light, to bring their teachings forward to common knowledge.

Dear Light Being know that - we understand Quantum Physics and Mechanics without studying them, we simply apply them in our manifestations. We do *not* have to accept anything or anyone in our lives, that do/es not make us happy or bring us forward on our spiritual path. Such Beings only drain our energies and hinder our development.

The more you walk in *your* Light, the more Light Beings you attract. (law of attraction) And do not be surprised that people and circumstances, which drained your energies, simply disappear from your life. Don't try to hold on to them, let go. They fulfill their own path and purpose for being.

Today I have the understanding that many of my experiences and Beings in my life, were sent as lessons to learn. I thank their higher self's for fulfilling their contract in assisting and reassuring me on my way. Without them, I would not have remembered, what I truly am – an immensely powerful Being of Light. I give thanks, for the many experiences and precious Light Beings, who crossed my life's path until today. In one way or another, each one allowed me an additional glimpse of the full meaning of BE!

I am certain a wealth of discoveries are yet to be made, before I *truly* understand, what I have been honored to bring forth…. I have found the most wonderful Light Beings that look/ed at me as their literal lifesaver, inspiration, guide, goddess, friend, adopted daughter, psychological help and life coach, when in fact *they* helped me on my own path – awaking ancient knowledge and my ET knowledge, getting clearer on understanding my path, and being open as a channel for the Light.

Only now I realize how much I missed seeing the colorful floating energies, auras of all living thing and Devas, which I used to see as a child. I re-discovered what I knew as a small child, I remember who I truly am.

My purpose for being here at this time, is to let my Light shine. Don't allow *anyone,* including yourself, to dim YOUR light. Shine and BE! Remember your purpose for incarnating at this time. Remember who you truly are. BE!

Lots of Light

Ruth Hildegard Henrich
Ambassador of Light

ACKNOWLEDGMENTS

I give special thanks to those Beings and energies who allowed me to see beyond human experiences and assisting me to remember through explicit visions

Lord Aemakshan leader from the Sirius galaxy, Magarethe Berg (my psychic grandmother), Mruhn Aht, Hildegardis (Saint Hildegard von Bingen)*who wants me to tell you that her books have been translated wrong by translators who interpreted her words with their limited understanding,* Pierre Richelieu, Mary Magdalene, Eleanor, Marie Antoinette, Isis, Nefertari, Brigit, Meruati, Asaneratu, Waleya, Ishti-n-iakja, Flamboyard Trisnian, the Atlantean scientists and the Lemurian energies with all their beautiful pictures, colors, scents and emotions awaking me through the touch of sound from the crystal organ and visions of the crystal mountains at the coast of California.

all those sparkling beings of pure energy
and ever changing form,
whose names do not translate into human sounds or
visible color range (light) –
the birds and sun rays have a better chance in
translating their names

and especially

the Beings of the mineral kingdom,
who never tire inviting me inside them
to copy knowledge on sub-atomic level,
and who show me their fascinating faces,
landscapes, pictures, sacred geometry and
relativity of time and space

channeled and experienced one-on-one with Source
by Ruth Hildegard Henrich

VISUAL CHANNELING'S

About my paintings
ART E FFECTS©

Dear Universe I am grateful for the experience of being passionate about everything beautiful and positive. Past life times are raising into consciousness, which is a wonderful experience. It happens in passionate expression of painting my memories in visual images, at least that which can be expressed this way. There are memories that need to be expressed by sound – so I sing and I cry.

I realize that as I am true to myself there are only good Beings and energies entering my life. I embrace my life and let go of the old, as it no longer will serve me in what is to come. Some of the coded visionary artwork by Ruth Hildegard Henrich is included in the channeled prayer book INTO THE LIGHT.

A complete book on my channeled visionary art will soon be published, as the coded information needs to be seen by many people. The contained codes will trigger memories in those who look at them.

The ASHANTARA keep instructing me to show this art. Due it's uniqueness, I have so far been unable to convince local galleries to show these unusual paintings (visionary art).

BE! seminars

BE! retreats and vacations

BE! healing sessions & nutrition seminars

BE! technology research

BE! DVDs and CDs

BE! cook books for children, students, newly weds & gourmets

BE! bumper stickers

BE! posters

BE! Diaries, journals, address & phone books

BE! notepads

BE! postcards

BE! Pens, paper weights

BE! engraved gem stones

BE! coffee mugs & glasses

BE! healing gem stone jewelry

BE! window art

BE! food supplements, drinking water

TEN PERCENT OF YOUR ORDER COST IS USED FOR RESEARCH
IN THE FIELDS OF:
drinking water generation
environment friendly products
and recoverable energies

to order products and for information write to:

www.RuthHenrichGroup.com
contact@RuthHenrichGroup.com

this page intentionally left blank

BY THE SAME AUTHOR

HEALING HOMES
How to create healthy living spaces
Cocoons for the soul
Healing spaces for Mother Earth
A guide for developers, city planners,
architects & interior designers

INTO THE LIGHT
Volume I
Prayers for transformation

Channeled prayers

VISIONS
Visions shown to Ruth Hildegard Henrich
during 2001 – 2008

TOP TOPP's
Do it yourself guide for hungry little stomachs
A children's cook book
by Ruth Hildegard Henrich
and Linda Bittner

ART E FFECTS
the visionary art of Ruth Hildegard Henrich
codes from the Ashantara
channeled paintings
1964 – 2008
by Ruth Hildegard Henrich

INDEX

Foreword 7-11

Introduction 12-14

I AM 15-16

The Ashantara 18

Channeled Change 19-20

Channeled Information 21-22

The Young Ones 23

Mineral Kingdom 24-25

Hieroglyphs I. 26

Bodies 27-33

Wake Up Call 34

Awakening I 38-39

Find and confirm yourself 40-43

Nourishment 44-48

Crystals 49-52

Being and Beings 53-57

Balancing Mother Earth 58-61

Mind Manipulation 62-64

About being human 65-67

How to be calm 68-70

Love each other as you love thyself 71-73

Sound Light Be! 74-76

Your Spectrum Colours 77-79

Awakening II 80-83

Hieroglyphs II 84-86

Shine your Light 87-91

Turbulence of Frequency Shifts 92-100

INDEX
Continued

Science 101-104
Medicine 105-106
Living 107-108
Relax – it is Law 109
Teachings and Preparation for Oneness 110-115
Touched by the Mountain Crystal 116
On Body 117-118
Learning to Be! 119-120
Final Words 122-123
Closing Words 124-125
Achknowledgements 126-127
Visual Channeling's 128
Availabe Products 129

NOTES